Descriptions fr

Selected from the books o

by Wendy Body

AR

GW01316381

Contents

Section 1

Section 2

Section 3

Longman

Edinburgh Gate
Harlow, Essex

The Hunters and the Hunted

On the ground below them stood the four enormous ducks, as tall as men, and three of them were holding guns in their hands. One had Mr Gregg's gun, one had Philip's gun, and one had William's gun.

The guns were all pointing right up at the nest.
"No! No! No!" called out Mr and Mrs Gregg, both together. "Don't shoot! Please don't shoot!"
"Why not?" said one of the ducks. It was the one who wasn't holding a gun. "You are always shooting at *us*."
"Oh, but that's not the same!" said Mr Gregg. "We are *allowed* to shoot ducks!"
"Who allows you?" asked the duck.
"We allow each other," said Mr Gregg.
"Very nice," said the duck. "And now *we* are going to allow each other to shoot you."

(I would have loved to have seen Mr Gregg's face just then.)

"Oh, *please*!" cried Mrs Greg. "My two little children are up here with us! You wouldn't shoot my *children*!"

"Yesterday you shot *my* children," said the duck. "You shot all six of my children."

"I'll never do it again!" cried Mr Gregg. "Never, never, never!"

"Do you really mean that?" asked the duck.

"I *do* mean it!" said Mr Gregg. "I'll never shoot another duck as long as I live!"

"That is not good enough," said the duck. "What about the deer?"

"I'll do anything you say if you will only put down those guns!" cried Mr Gregg. "I'll never shoot another duck or another deer or anything else again!"

"Will you give me your word on that?" said the duck.

"I will! I will!" said Mr Gregg.

"Will you throw away your guns?" asked the duck.

"I will break them into tiny bits!" said Mr Gregg. "And never again need you be afraid of me or my family."

From *The Magic Finger*

Four Sticky Little Boys

On one Tuesday evening after Mr Twit had been up the ladder and smeared the tree with HUGTIGHT, four little boys crept into the garden to look at the monkeys. They didn't care about the thistles and stinging-nettles, not when there were monkeys to look at. After a while, they got tired of looking at the monkeys, so they explored further into the garden and found the ladder leaning against The Big Dead Tree. They decided to climb up it just for fun.

There's nothing wrong with that.

The next morning, when Mr Twit went out to collect the birds, he found four miserable little boys sitting in the tree, stuck as tight as could be by the seats of their pants to the branches. There were no birds because the presence of the boys had scared them away.

Mr Twit was furious.

"As there are no birds for my pie tonight," he shouted, "then it'll have to be *boys* instead!" He started to climb the ladder. "Boy Pie might be better than Bird Pie," he went on, grinning horribly. "More meat and not so many tiny little bones!"

The boys were terrified. "He's going to boil us!" cried one of them.
"He'll stew us alive!" wailed the second one.
"He'll cook us with carrots!" cried the third.
But the fourth little boy, who had more sense than the others, whispered, "Listen, I've just had an idea. We are only stuck *by the seats of our pants*. So quick! Unbutton your pants and slip out of them and fall to the ground."

Mr Twit had reached the top of the ladder and was just about to make a grab for the nearest boy when they all suddenly tumbled out of the tree and ran for home with their naked bottoms winking at the sun.

From *The Twits*

The Witching Hour

Sophie couldn't sleep.

A brilliant moonbeam was slanting through a gap in the curtains. It was shining right on to her pillow.

The other children in the dormitory had been asleep for hours.

Sophie closed her eyes and lay quite still. She tried very hard to doze off.

It was no good. The moonbeam was like a silver blade slicing through the room on to her face.

The house was absolutely silent. No voices came up from downstairs. There were no footsteps on the floor either.

The window behind the curtain was wide open, but nobody was walking on the pavement outside. No cars went by on the street. Not the tiniest sound could be heard anywhere. Sophie had never known such silence.

Perhaps, she told herself, this was what they called the witching hour.

The witching hour, somebody had once whispered to her, was a special moment in the middle of the night when every child and every grown-up was in a deep deep sleep, and all the dark things came out from hiding and had the world to themselves.

The moonbeam was brighter than ever on Sophie's pillow. She decided to get out of bed and close the gap in the curtains.

You got punished if you were caught out of bed after lights-out. Even if you said you had to go to the lavatory, that was not accepted as an excuse and they punished you just the same. But there was no one about now, Sophie was sure of that.

She reached out for her glasses that lay on the chair beside her bed. They had steel rims and very thick lenses, and she could hardly see a thing without them. She put them on, then she slipped out of bed and tip-toed over to the window.

When she reached the curtains, Sophie hesitated. She longed to duck underneath them and lean out of the window to see what the world looked like now that the witching hour was at hand.

She listened again. Everywhere it was deathly still.

The longing to look out became so strong she couldn't resist it. Quickly, she ducked under the curtains and leaned out of the window.

In the silvery moonlight, the village street she knew so well seemed completely different. The houses looked bent and crooked, like houses in a fairy tale. Everything was pale and ghostly and milky-white.

Across the road, she could see Mrs Rance's shop, where you bought buttons and wool and bits of elastic. It didn't look real. There was something dim and misty about that too.

Sophie allowed her eye to travel further and further down the street.

Suddenly she froze. *There was something coming up the street on the opposite side.*

It was something black …

Something tall and black …

Something very tall and very black and very thin.

It wasn't human. It couldn't be. It was four times as tall as the tallest human. It was so tall its head was higher than the upstairs windows of the houses. Sophie opened her mouth to scream, but no sound came out. Her throat, like her whole body, was frozen with fright.

This was the witching hour all right.

The tall black figure was coming her way. It was keeping very close to the houses across the street, hiding in the shadowy places where there was no moonlight.

On and on it came, nearer and nearer. But it was moving in spurts. It would stop, then it would move on, then it would stop again.

But what on earth was it doing?

Ah-ha! Sophie could see now what it was up to. It was stopping in front of each house. It would stop and peer into the upstairs window of each house in the street. It actually had to bend down to peer into the upstairs windows. That's how tall it was.

It would stop and peer in. Then it would slide on to the next house and stop again, and peer in, and so on all along the street.

It was much closer now and Sophie could see it more clearly.

Looking at it carefully, she decided it had to be some kind of PERSON.

A GIANT PERSON, perhaps.

Sophie stared hard across the misty moonlit street. The Giant (if that was what he was) was wearing a long BLACK CLOAK.

In one hand he was holding what looked like a VERY LONG, THIN TRUMPET.

In the other hand, he held a LARGE SUITCASE.

The Giant had stopped now right in front of Mr and Mrs Goochey's house. The Goocheys had a greengrocer's shop in the middle of the High Street, and the family lived above the shop. The two Goochey children slept in the upstairs front room, Sophie knew that.

The Giant was peering through the window into the room where Michael and Jane Goochey were sleeping. From across the street, Sophie watched and held her breath.

From *The BFG*

Home

When I was four months old, my mother died suddenly and my father was left to look after me all by himself. This is how I looked at the time.

I had no brothers or sisters.

So all through my boyhood, from the age of four months onward, there were just the two of us, my father and me.

We lived in an old gipsy caravan behind a filling-station. My father owned the filling-station and the caravan and a small field behind, but that was about all he owned in the world. It was a very small filling-station on a small country road surrounded by fields and woody hills.

While I was still a baby, my father washed me and fed me and changed my nappies and did all the millions of other things a mother normally does for her child. That is not an easy task for a man, especially when he has to earn his living at the same time by repairing motor-car engines and serving customers with petrol.

But my father didn't seem to mind. I think that all the love he had felt for my mother when she was alive he now lavished upon me. During my early years, I never had a moment's unhappiness or illness and here I am on my fifth birthday.

I was now a scruffy little boy as you can see, with grease and oil all over me, but that was because I spent all day in the workshop helping my father with the cars.

The filling-station itself had only two pumps. There was a wooden shed behind the pumps that served as an office. There was nothing in the office except an old table and a cash register to put the money into. It was one of those where you pressed a button and a bell rang and the drawer shot out with a terrific bang. I used to love that.

The square brick building to the right of the office was the workshop. My father built that himself with loving care, and it was the only really solid thing in the place.

"We are engineers, you and I," he used to say to me. "We earn our living by repairing engines and we can't do good work in a rotten workshop." It was a fine workshop, big enough to take one car comfortably and leave plenty of room round the sides for working. It had a telephone so that customers could arrange to bring their cars in for repair.

The caravan was our house and our home. It was a real old gipsy wagon with big wheels and fine patterns painted all over it in yellow and red and blue. My father said it was at least a hundred and fifty years old. Many gipsy children, he said, had been born in it and had grown up within its wooden walls. With a horse to pull it, the old caravan must have wandered for thousands of miles along the roads

and lanes of England. But now its wanderings were over, and because the wooden spokes in the wheels were beginning to rot, my father had propped it up underneath with bricks.

There was only one room in the caravan and it wasn't much bigger than a fair-sized modern bathroom. It was a narrow room, the shape of the caravan itself, and against the back wall were two bunk beds, one above the other. The top one was my father's, the bottom one mine.

Although we had electric lights in the workshop, we were not allowed to have them in the caravan. The electricity people said it was unsafe to put wires into something as old and rickety as that. So we got our heat and light in much the same way as the gipsies had done years ago. There was a wood-burning stove with a chimney that went up through the roof, and this kept us warm in winter. There was a paraffin burner on which to boil a kettle or cook a stew, and there was a paraffin lamp hanging from the ceiling.

When I needed a bath, my father would heat a kettle of water and pour it into a basin. Then he would strip me naked and scrub me all over, standing up. This, I think, got me just as clean as if I were washed in a bath – probably cleaner because I didn't finish up sitting in my own dirty water.

For furniture, we had two chairs and a small table, and those, apart from a tiny chest of drawers, were all the home comforts we possessed. They were all we needed.

The lavatory was a funny little wooden hut standing in the field some way behind the caravan. It was fine in summertime, but I can tell you that sitting out there on a snowy day in winter was like sitting in a fridge.

Immediately behind the caravan was an old apple tree. It bore lovely apples that ripened in the middle of September and you could go on picking them for the next four or five weeks. Some of the boughs of the tree hung right over the caravan and when the wind blew the apples down in the night they often landed on our roof. I would hear them going *thump … thump … thump …* above my head as I lay in my bunk, but those noises never frightened me because I knew exactly what was making them.

I really loved living in that gipsy caravan. I loved it especially in the evenings when I was tucked up in my bunk and my father was telling me stories. The paraffin lamp was turned low, and I could see lumps of wood glowing red-hot in the old stove and wonderful it was to be lying there snug and warm in my bunk in that little room. Most wonderful of all was the feeling that when I went to sleep, my father would still be there, very close to me, sitting in his chair by the fire, or lying in the bunk above my own.

From *Danny The Champion of the World*

The Tunnel

Hungry and trembling, James stood alone out in the open, wondering what to do. The night was all around him now, and high overhead a wild white moon was riding in the sky. There was not a sound, not a movement anywhere.

Most people – and especially small children – are often quite scared of being out of doors alone in the moonlight. Everything is so deadly quiet, and the shadows are so long and black, and they keep turning into strange shapes that seem to move as you look at them, and the slightest little snap of a twig makes you jump.

James felt exactly like that now. He stared straight ahead with large frightened eyes, hardly daring to breathe. Not far away, in the middle of the garden, he could see the giant peach towering over everything else. Surely it was even bigger tonight than ever before? And what a dazzling sight it was! The moonlight was shining and glinting on its great curving sides, turning them to crystal and silver. It looked like a tremendous silver ball lying there in the grass, silent, mysterious, and wonderful.

And then all at once, little shivers of excitement started running over the skin on James's back.

Something else, he told himself, *something stranger than ever this time, is about to happen to me again soon.* He was sure of it. He could feel it coming.

He looked around him, wondering what on earth it was going to be. The garden lay soft and silver in the moonlight. The grass was wet with dew and a million dewdrops were sparkling and twinkling like diamonds around his feet. And now suddenly, the whole place, the whole garden seemed to be *alive* with magic.

Almost without knowing what he was doing, as though drawn by some powerful magnet, James Henry Trotter started walking slowly towards the giant peach. He climbed over the fence that surrounded it, and stood directly beneath it, staring up at its great bulging sides.

He put out a hand and touched it gently with the tip of one finger. It felt soft and warm and slightly furry, like the skin of a baby mouse. He moved a step closer and rubbed his cheek lightly against the soft skin. And then suddenly, while he was doing this, he happened to notice that right beside him and below him, close to the ground, there was a hole in the side of the peach.

It was quite a large hole, the sort of thing an animal about the size of a fox might have made.

James knelt down in front of it, and poked his head and shoulders inside.

He crawled in.

He kept on crawling.

This isn't a hole, he thought excitedly. *It's a tunnel!*

The tunnel was damp and murky, and all around him there was the curious bittersweet smell of fresh peach. The floor was soggy under his knees, the walls were wet and sticky, and peach juice was dripping from the ceiling. James opened his mouth and caught some of it on his tongue. It tasted delicious.

He was crawling uphill now, as though the tunnel were leading straight towards the very centre of the gigantic fruit. Every few seconds he paused and took a bite out of the wall. The peach flesh was sweet and juicy, and marvellously refreshing.

He crawled on for several more yards, and then suddenly – *bang* – the top of his head bumped into something extremely hard blocking his way. He glanced up. In front of him there was a solid wall that seemed at first as though it were made of wood. He touched it with his fingers. It certainly felt like wood, except that it was very jagged and full of deep grooves.

"Good heavens!" he said. "I know what this is! I've come to the stone in the middle of the peach!" Then he noticed that there was a small door cut into the face of the peach stone. He gave a push.

It swung open. He crawled through it, and before he had time to glance up and see where he was, he heard a voice saying, "Look who's here!" And another one said, "We've been *waiting* for you!"

James stopped and stared at the speakers, his face white with horror.

He started to stand up, but his knees were shaking so much he had to sit down again on the floor. He glanced behind him, thinking he could bolt back into the tunnel the way he had come, but the doorway had disappeared. There was now only a solid brown wall behind him.

James' large frightened eyes travelled slowly round the room.

The creatures, some sitting on a chair, others reclining on a sofa, were all watching him intently.

Creatures?

Or were they insects?

An insect is usually something rather small, is it not? A grasshopper, for example, is an insect.

So what would you call it if you saw a grasshopper as large as a dog? As large as a *large* dog. You could hardly call *that* an insect, could you?

There was an Old-Green-Grasshopper as large as a large dog sitting directly across the room from James now.

And next to the Old-Green-Grasshopper, there was an enormous Spider.

And next to them, there was a giant Ladybird with nine black spots on her scarlet shell.

These three were squatting upon a magnificent chair.

On a sofa near by, reclining comfortably in curled-up positions, there were a Centipede and an Earthworm.

On the floor over in the far corner, there was something thick and white that looked as though it might be a Silkworm. But it was sleeping soundly and nobody was paying any attention to it.

Every one of these "creatures" was at least as big as James himself, and in the strange greenish light that shone down from somewhere in the ceiling, they were absolutely terrifying to behold.

From *James and the Giant Peach*

Mr Willy Wonka

Mr Wonka was standing all alone just inside the open gates of the factory.

And what an extraordinary little man he was!

He had a black top hat on his head. He wore a tail coat made of a beautiful plum-coloured velvet. His trousers were bottle green. His gloves were pearly grey. And in one hand he carried a fine gold-topped walking cane.

Covering his chin, there was a small, neat, pointed black beard – a goatee. And his eyes – his eyes were most marvellously bright. They seemed to be sparkling and twinkling at you all the time. The whole face, in fact, was alight with fun and laughter.

And oh, how clever he looked! How quick and sharp and full of life! He kept making quick jerky little movements with his head, cocking it this way and that, and taking everything in with those bright twinkling eyes. He was like a squirrel in the quickness of his movements, like a quick clever old squirrel from the park.

Suddenly, he did a funny little skipping dance in the snow, and he spread his arms wide, and he smiled at the five children.

"Here we are!" cried Mr Wonka, trotting along in front of the group. "Through this big red door, please! *That's* right! It's nice and warm inside! I have to keep it warm inside the factory because of the workers! My workers are used to an extremely hot climate! They can't stand the cold! They'd perish if they went outdoors in this weather! They'd freeze to death!"

"But who *are* these workers?" asked Augustus Gloop.

"All in good time, my dear boy!" said Mr Wonka, smiling at Augustus. "Be patient! You shall see everything as we go along! Are all of you inside? Good! Would you mind closing he door? Thank you!"

Charlie Bucket found himself standing in a long corridor that stretched away in front of him as far as he could see. The corridor was so wide that a car could easily have been driven along it. The walls were pale pink, the lighting was soft and pleasant.

"How lovely and warm!" whispered Charlie.

"I know. And what a marvellous smell!" answered Grandpa Joe, taking a long deep sniff. All the most wonderful smells in the world seemed to be mixed up in the air around them – the smell of roasting coffee and burnt sugar and melting chocolate and mint and violets and crushed hazelnuts and apple blossom and caramel and lemon peel …

And far away in the distance, from the heart of the great factory, came a muffled roar of energy as though some monstrous gigantic machine were spinning its wheels at breakneck speed.

"Now *this*, my dear children," said Mr Wonka, raising his voice above the noise, "this is the main corridor. Will you please hang your coats and hats on those pegs over there, and then follow me. That's the way! Good! Everyone ready! Come on, then! Here we go!" He trotted off rapidly down the corridor with the tails of his plum-coloured velvet coat flapping behind him, and the visitors all hurried after him.

It was quite a large party of people, when you came to think of it. There were nine grown-ups and five children, fourteen in all. So you can imagine that there was a good deal of pushing and shoving as they hustled and bustled down the passage, trying to keep up with the swift little figure in front of them.

"Come *on*!" cried Mr Wonka. "Get a move on, please! We'll never get round today if you dawdle like this!" Soon, he turned right off the main corridor into another slightly narrower passage.

Then he turned left.

Then left again.

Then right.

Then left.

Then right.

Then right.

Then left.

The place was like a gigantic rabbit warren, with passages leading this way and that in every direction.

"Don't you let go of my hand, Charlie," whispered Grandpa Joe.
"Notice how all these passages are sloping downwards!" called out Mr Wonka. "We are now going underground! *All* the most important rooms in my factory are deep down below the surface!"
"Why is that?" somebody asked.
"There wouldn't be *nearly* enough space for them up on top!" answered Mr Wonka. "These rooms we are going to see are *enormous*! They're larger than football fields! No building in the *world* would be big enough to house them! But down here, underneath the ground. I've got *all* the space I want. There's no limit – so long as I hollow it out."

Mr Wonka turned right.

He turned left.

He turned right again.

The passages were sloping steeper and steeper downhill now.

Then suddenly, Mr Wonka stopped. In front of him, there was a shiny metal door. The party crowded round. On the door, in large letters it said:

THE CHOCOLATE ROOM

"An important room, this!" cried Mr Wonka, taking a bunch of keys from his pocket and slipping one into the keyhole of the door. "*This* is the nerve centre of the whole factory, the heart of the whole business! And so *beautiful*! I *insist* upon my rooms being beautiful! I can't *abide* ugliness in factories! *In* we go, then! But *do* be careful, my dear children! Don't lose your heads! Don't get over-excited! Keep very calm!"

Mr Wonka opened the door. Five children and nine grown-ups pushed their ways in – and *oh*, what an amazing sight it was that now met their eyes!

They were looking down upon a lovely valley. There were green meadows on either side of the valley, and along the bottom of it there flowed a great brown river.

What is more, there was a tremendous waterfall halfway along the river – a steep cliff over which the water curled and rolled in a solid sheet, and then went crashing down into a boiling churning whirlpool of froth and spray.

From *Charlie and the Chocolate Factory*

A Kind of Electricity

Slowly Matilda sat down. Oh, the rottenness of it all! The unfairness! How dare they expel her for something she hadn't done!

Matilda felt herself getting angrier … and angrier … and angrier … so unbearably angry that something was bound to explode inside her very soon.

The newt was still squirming in the tall glass of water. It looked horribly uncomfortable. The glass was not big enough for it. Matilda glared at the Trunchbull. How she hated her. She glared at the glass with the newt in it. She longed to march up and grab the glass and tip the contents, newt and all, over the Trunchbull's head. She trembled to think what the Trunchbull would do to her if she did that.

The Trunchbull was sitting behind the teacher's table staring with a mixture of horror and fascination at the newt wriggling in the glass. Matilda's eyes were also riveted on the glass. And now, quite slowly, there began to creep over Matilda a most extraordinary and peculiar feeling. The feeling was mostly in the eyes. A kind of electricity seemed to be gathering inside them. A sense of power was brewing in those eyes of hers, a feeling of great strength was settling itself deep inside her eyes. But there was also another feeling which was something else altogether, and which she could not understand. It was like flashes of lightning. Little waves of lightning seemed to be flashing out of her eyes. Her eyeballs were beginning to get hot, as though vast energy was building up somewhere inside them. It was an amazing sensation. She kept her eyes steadily on the glass, and now the power was concentrating itself in one small part of each eye and growing stronger and stronger and it felt as though millions of tiny little invisible arms with hands on them were shooting out of her eyes towards the glass she was staring at.

"*Tip it!*" Matilda whispered. "*Tip it over!*" She saw the glass wobble. It actually tilted backwards a fraction of an inch, then righted itself again. She kept pushing at it with all those millions of invisible little

arms and hands that were reaching out from her eyes, feeling the power that was flashing straight from the two little black dots in the very centres of her eyeballs.
"*Tip it!*" she whispered again. "*Tip it over!*"

Once more the glass wobbled. She pushed harder still, willing her eyes to shoot out more power. And then, very very slowly, so slowly she could hardly see it happening, the glass began to lean backwards, farther and farther and farther backwards until it was balancing on just one edge of its base. And there it teetered for a few seconds before finally toppling over and falling with a sharp tinkle on to the desk-top. The water in it and the squirming newt splashed out all over Miss Trunchbull's enormous bosom. The headmistress let out a yell that must have rattled every window-pane in the building and for the second time in the last five minutes she shot out of her chair like a rocket. The newt clutched desperately at the cotton smock where it covered the great chest and there it clung with its little claw-like feet. The Trunchbull looked down and saw it and she bellowed even louder and with a swipe of her hand she sent the creature flying across the class-room. It landed on the floor beside Lavender's desk and very quickly she ducked down and picked it up and put it into her pencil-box for another time. A newt, she decided, was a useful thing to have around.

The Trunchbull, her face more like a boiled ham than ever, was standing before the class quivering with fury. Her massive bosom was heaving in and out and the splash of water down the front of it made a dark wet patch that had probably soaked right through to her skin.

"*Who did it?*" she roared. "*Come on! Own up! Step forward! You won't escape this time! Who is responsible for this dirty job? Who pushed over this glass?*"

Nobody answered. The whole room remained silent as a tomb.

"Matilda!" she roared. "It was you! I know it was you!" Matilda, in the second row, sat very still and said nothing. A strange feeling of serenity and confidence was sweeping over her and all of a sudden she found that she was frightened by nobody in the world. With the power of her eyes alone she had compelled a glass of water to tip and spill its contents over the horrible Headmistress, and anybody who could do that could do anything.

"Speak up, you clotted carbuncle!" roared the Trunchbull. "Admit that you did it!" Matilda looked right back into the flashing eyes of this infuriated female giant and said with total calmness, "I have not moved away from my desk, Miss Trunchbull, since the lesson began. I can say no more."

Suddenly the entire class seemed to rise up against the Headmistress.

"She didn't move!" they cried out. "Matilda didn't move! Nobody moved! You must have knocked it over yourself!"

"I most certainly did not knock it over myself!" roared the Trunchbull. "How dare you suggest a thing like that! Speak up, Miss Honey! You must have seen everything! Who knocked over my glass?"

"None of the children did, Miss Trunchbull," Miss Honey answered. "I can vouch for it that nobody has moved from his or her desk all the time you've been here, except for Nigel and he has not moved from his corner."

Miss Trunchbull glared at Miss Honey. Miss Honey met her gaze without flinching.

"I am telling you the truth, Headmistress," she said. "You must have knocked it over without knowing it. That sort of thing is easy to do."

"I am fed up with you useless bunch of midgets!" roared the Trunchbull. "I refuse to waste any more of my precious time in here!" And with that she marched out of the class-room, slamming the door behind her.

In the stunned silence that followed, Miss Honey walked up to the front of the class and stood behind her table.

"Phew!" she said. "I think we've had enough school for one day, don't you? The class is dismissed. You may all go out into the playground and wait for your parents to come and take you home."

From *Matilda*